To Mr.

May your ... be filled with love. you & your wife daily & may your purposes be complete in the earth individually & collectively. love one another always unconditionally 'til death do you part.

Love Always
Fiona James

MW01137952

FIONA JAMES

Marry the One Who...

Copyright © 2019 Fiona James

All rights reserved.

ISBN: 9781795649988
Imprint: Independently published

DEDICATION

This book is dedicated to every person who has loved and lost, loved and won as well as those still hopeful. #hopefulromantic

...

CONTENTS

...

ACKNOWLEDGMENTS

The completion of this project would not have been possible without God first and foremost. So, I honor Him greatly for gracing me through this process even with the bumps in the road, downfalls, moments of insanity (LOL) but loving me so much that I can write about love.

Secondly, to my family who supports me in everything! My parents Bishop Andrew and Connie James, Sr., always taught me to release the limits and give God control and with God ALL things are possible. I am blessed to have you as parents as it is through your example of love and perseverance that I have the example of a God covenant and love. To my siblings, Angela (Greg), Andrew Jr. (Tequita) and Desiree, I love y'all beyond words. Thank you for not letting me do anything in mediocrity. Y'all keep me together. Your love, prayers and support mean the world to me.

To my beautiful daughter, Paris, you taught me how to love on another level and motivate me to be greater and be better. I am proud of you every day! Keep pushing and never give up. Always place God first! Remember the rule still applies... Age 74 (LOL) Mama loves you!!!

To my best friend for life and Editor Kyle Alexander (Habakkuk Transcriptions), thank you for keeping me focused on me and this project even when I lost focus or would not listen. You have this way of whipping me back into shape. LOL This project would not be finished if it wasn't for you.

i

To my Rapture Ready Productions family, y'all really made this project come to life. Thanks to Jeremy Duncan (CEO) for love, support and encouragement for as long as I have known you but specifically for allowing me to use the Rapture Ready team to complete this project.

Keion Givens, you are a beast and really came through on the design cover and gave my vision life! In spite of my draft of expression (which was horrible), you managed to give it life and substance. You are genius!

Avril Moore aka Po3tic Goddess I am honored to have you featured on the EP with your poem "Marital Views" You did not disappoint! I appreciate your gift and am grateful to call you Sis!

To Jason Knighten aka JayKnight, you did your "real good" mixing and mastering on this project and really came through with heart on your track. I am honored to be featured with you. Thanks for the prayers and pushing!

To everyone from Rapture Ready, thank y'all for the love! Y'all supported me in words and deeds. Your constant drive and tenacity motivates me.

Jeremiah Stewart you jumped on this project and took off from PR to promo and beyond. Your humility is breath taking and I am blessed to have connected with you in this season

To every person who has loved and supported me... Y'all rock! Thank you!

Other marriage inspirations...

Bishop Raymond and First Lady Mildred Johnson, Pastor Wuan and LaKeisha Miller, Pastor William and Maria Bates, Min. James & Janice Rooks., Min. Charles & Gwendolyn Guillory, Warren & Cynthia Simmons, Min. Kevin & Sandra Haynes, Sr., Donald & Joy Robins, Sr., Gregory & Angela Jenkins, Dameon & Nakisha Roberson, Jessie & Sonceree Grisby, Timothy and Tina Turner, Curtis & Raena Bolton, Hubert & Eartha Domingue, Andrew & Tequita James, Kendrick & Brittany Hinyard, Joseph & Lisa Hughes, Cecil & Tenisha Moore, Maricio & Queena Leach, Terrance & Jhane Wilcox, Stephen & Angele Anson, your example of unity, partnership, support and love towards one another is inspiring. You bless so many in how you love one another and that love blesses me to be a witness. Thank you!!!

To my "babies" entering into marriage Kevin Haynes & Latoya Gage and Henry Harris and Kierra Haynes...

Your love for Christ and how you make the decision to serve Him wholeheartedly will shine through your love for one another. Keep God first and remember His love and rely on it to access the love you will have for one another for as long as you shall live as husband and wife. Love you all!!!

•••

Introduction

God is LOVE!!! He formed this world and created every being out of that LOVE. So, it would be remiss of Him to not want us to experience that love in its fullest capacity. God has blessed us with the gift of marriage to experience love and covenant in the manner in which He has with us. He created it and it is a good thing, it brings Him glory and is meant to last forever (Proverbs 18:22, Colossians 1:16, Isaiah 43:6-7). Marriages can be tumultuous and it takes work but marriage is supposed to bless and honor God.

I had the privilege of growing up in a home where both of my parents exemplified the love of God towards one another as well as my siblings and I. Was it a perfect love? Of course not. But they loved as best as they knew how and never gave up on that love. From high school sweethearts, now forty-three years later, their love has stood the test of times with private and some public battles but they withstood those times together. God's love is the only PERFECT LOVE but it is an amazing experience when two people come together to create a semi-perfect love in the image of God. It is the story of my parents that the nuggets throughout this book are written and through their example of love that "Marry the One Who..." was birthed. This book is in no way a guarantee that love will work out perfectly for you based on these nuggets for I do believe that only the guidance of God can do that but hopefully it will help in your selections as well as ultimately marriage.

...

IN THE BEGINNING
ADAM AND EVE

THE FOUNDATION OF THE WORLD STEMS FROM THE LOVE OF OUR GOD. HE CREATED ALL THINGS FROM NOTHING BUT EVERYTHING IS CREATED IN LOVE.

GOD CREATED EVE FROM THE RIB OF ADAM BECAUSE HE DID NOT WANT ADAM TO BE ALONE. IN THE BEGINNING, GOD DISPLAYED HIS LOVE FOR THAT WHICH HE CREATED AND KNEW THE IMPORTANCE OF ADAM FEELING THAT SAME LOVE FROM ANOTHER OTHER THAN HE, HIMSELF. GOD IS A RELATIONAL GOD AND HAS CREATED THIS WORLD TO HAVE FRIENDSHIPS, RELATIONSHIPS, FAMILY AND LOVE FOR ALL MANKIND. ADAM AND EVE'S CREATION WAS AN EXAMPLE OF THE COVENANT BETWEEN HUSBAND AND WIFE. IT DISPLAYS LOVE ETERNAL EVEN THROUGH FAULT. FOR BETTER OR WORSE, RICHER OR POORER, SICKNESS AND HEALTH, TIL DEATH DO US PART.

WE HAVE TO SET THE STANDARD - WE WERE GIVEN THE HIGHEST PLACE OF RULERSHIP AND RESPONSIBILITY TO REFLECT GOD ON EARTH WITH LOVE. THOUGH GOD'S LOVE IS PERFECT, OURS MAY NOT ALWAYS BE SO WE SHOULD RELY ON HIS LOVE AS GUIDANCE.

THERE IS PURPOSE IN UNIFORMITY OF LOVE ESPECIALLY BETWEEN A MAN AND WOMAN! WE SHOULD DAILY BE SEEKING GOD IN OUR SINGLENESS, DATING ENCOUNTERS AND MARRIAGE. IT IS THROUGH HIS GUIDANCE THAT WE WILL NEVER BE LED ASTRAY. OUR RELATIONAL SITUATIONS SHOULD MIMIC GOD'S INTENTIONS OF LOVE ALWAYS.

YOUR RELATIONSHIP SHAPES YOUR REFLECTION OF LOVE!!! THAT REFLECTION SHOULD ALWAYS BE GOD!!!

A Prayer for Unity in Marriage

Heavenly Father we come before you to thank you for all you have done and continue to do in our lives and marriage. We come before you today, God, asking for a stronger bond of unity in our marriage covenant.

Father we ask that you will give us the ability to be a united front for you letting nothing come between us. Help us, Father to identify and work through anything that is not pleasing to you so we can continually reach higher levels of unity in our marriage – spiritually, physically, and mentally.

We are thankful and excited to see the work of your hand as we do our best to seek your face daily. We love you and thank you for all of these things. In Jesus' name we pray. Amen!

"Make every effort to keep yourselves united in the Spirit, binding yourselves together with peace." (Ephesians 4:3 NLT)

crosswalk.com

MARRY THE ONE WHO SEEKS GOD ABOUT WAYS TO LOVE YOU

JAMES 1:5 KJV

5 If any of you lack wisdom, let him ask of God, that giveth to all men liberally, and upbraideth not; and it shall be given him.

Having the ability to recognize your need for guidance with every detail of your life is critical especially when it involves a forever mate. But prior to and after you have been blessed with someone hopefully that need to seek counsel from god on how to love as he loves will be a constant in your life.

MARRY THE ONE WHO RECOGNIZES THE DEVILS ATTACK ON YOU AND RATHER THAN ASSIST THE DEVIL, THEY GO INTO SPIRITUAL WAR ON YOUR BEHALF.

EPHESIANS 6:18 KJV

[18] Praying always with all prayer and supplication in the Spirit, and watching thereunto with all perseverance and supplication for all saints.

Praying for one another is not only necessary but biblical. To be able to constantly intercede in prayer is one of the purest forms of love and it draws each person closer to the other.

MARRY THE ONE THAT WILL WORK OUT WITH YOU AND FEED YOU SPICY HOG HEAD CHEESE WITH A HONEY BUN AND AMERICAN CHEESE WHEN YOU DO A GOOD JOB.

It's okay to have disciplines within your relationships. Actually, I believe it's needed but I also believe that if that's all you have then it leaves no room for fun. No fun leads to dull and boring and the enemy can find his way in those vulnerable moments. Live a little!!! Eat a honey bun while dieting. Lol

MARRY THE ONE WHO WILL LOVE YOU WITHOUT LIMITS OR EXCUSES

1 PETER 4:8 KJV
8And above all things have fervent charity among yourselves: for charity shall cover the multitude of sins.

A person who can love you to the extreme exemplifies true love. They see the real you, when there's no façade or pretend. They see the part of you that you hide from the world and yet they love you anyway. They love you unapologetically.

MARRY THE ONE WHO WILL LOVE THE SAVED & SANCTIFIED YOU AS WELL AS THE RAW AND RATCHET.
#WEALLGOTSOMERATCHERINUS

LUKE 6:32-42 KJV
(VS. 36-37)

36 Be ye therefore merciful, as your Father also is merciful. 37 Judge not, and ye shall not be judged: condemn not, and ye shall not be condemned: forgive, and ye shall be forgiven:

It speaks to the life of every person even those now saved. Every person has a past and there are a lot of things that are not proud moments. One of the greatest gifts is being able to love the person based on their past, present and what god will do in the future. Loving the human side of them before you ever meet the spiritual side is commendable.

MARRY THE ONE WHO WILL WATCH YOUR FAVORITE SHOWS AGAINST THEIR OWN DESIRE JUST TO SPEND TIME ALONE WITH YOU
{NETFLIX & CHILL OR NAH?}

PHILIPPIANS 2:3 KJV
³ Let nothing be done through strife or vainglory; but in lowliness of mind let each esteem other better than themselves.

Many men despise lifetime or the hallmark channel just as many women would prefer not to watch sports every week. But the true art of love is compromise. Being able to put aside personal dislikes appeasing your partner, takes on a form of selflessness beyond words. It's about quality time not what's actually being done during that time. Let love live!

MARRY THE ONE WHO POURS JUST AS MUCH INTO YOU AS YOU DO THEM

LUKE 6:38 KJV

[38] Give, and it shall be given unto you; good measure, pressed down, and shaken together, and running over, shall men give into your bosom. For with the same measure that ye mete withal it shall be measured to you again.

Reciprocity begins and ends with a giving heart. Each day should be one where you strive to out give the one you love. The more time you spend finding ways to love them more, please them more should be a daily goal set. They will speak life into you and uplift you.

MARRY THE ONE WHO WILL SHARE EVERY PART OF THEIR LIFE WITH NOT JUST THE PIECES THAT'S CONVENIENT FOR THEM.

If the you can share the most intimate moments of your life in honesty, a forever bond can be established. It's in those pieces that agape love is formed and an understanding that surpasses understanding. Create a space that's safe to be completely transparent and there be no judgment. Even with the beautiful pieces a support factor is created and love can flourish and grow. The good and the bad has its rewards.

MARRY THE ONE WHO IS SELFLESS.

1 CORINTHIANS 13:5 KJV
5 Doth not behave itself unseemly, seeketh
not her own, is not easily provoked,
thinketh no evil.

I will give my all with no expectation
of a return because I love you just
that much. Those things I do, I give
will come from a place that only has
you in mind. I will give more with
no thought of myself for I do know
that you will do the same. There we
find a selfless kind of love that will
transcend time.

MARRY THE ONE THAT CALLS YOU FOR NOTHING OTHER THAN TO HEAR YOUR VOICE.

Aside from the voice of God, their voice should exude peace to your soul. Even in those moments of discourse, the sound of their voice should still cause a quiver down your spine. Even if it's the air from the breaths they take, their voice should take your breath away. Check in periodically throughout the day just to hear that voice that lets you know...

I got you no matter what!

MARRY THE ONE WHO'S HEARD YOU SNORE LIKE A GORILLA BUT SAYS I WAS SOUND ASLEEP OR TEASES YOU. OR, HEARD YOU PASS GAS IN YOUR SLEEP BUT DECIDED TO STAY. THEY ARE THE REAL MVP.

We all have something that may not be the most attractive but when you truly love someone, you overlook those things because who they truly are is far greater than that something. You get to see them for who they are even with all the quirks and love them and laugh at them. The fun part is just coming out and saying, "hey! I snore! And you're gonna love every bit of it."

MARRY THE ONE WHO NEVER MAKES YOU QUESTION THEIR LOVE OR LOYALTY

One of the hardest things is overcoming past hurts and disappointments but being able to recognize that we all have situations from a certain time in life that brought about insecurities of makes everyone questionable. To be patient and navigate through those moments are rare but the ones who master this skill will find that it can create an opportunity to learn more about the other person and opens the door for you both to heal and work at being better for one another – whatever it take.

MARRY THE ONE WHO SAYS "I GOT YOU" AND FOLLOWS THROUGH

If on your worst day, they keep on loving you, if you're struggling and they reach out to lend a helping hand, if they are going through and still consider you, then you have someone solid. Hold onto that person. Good people are hard to find.

MARRY THE ONE WHO TRULY LOVES GOD

How will they know how to love you if they understand god's love and his thoughts towards you? But the one who chases after god and learns how he loves us and how he wants us to love one another will most assuredly know how to love you completely and eternally!!!

21

MARRY THE ONE WHO ONLY SPEAKS WHAT THE WORD OF GOD SAYS ABOUT YOU, OVER YOU

As the previous mt1 stated, one can only speak what god says if they are aware of what god says. They will never speak ill words over your life even in the greatest of disagreements. They will constantly be reminded of who god has called you to be and speak to that person in you even when you are not acting as such. Love and life should always be the course of words spoken.

MARRY THE ONE WHO CREATES TIME FOR YOU #ITMATTERS #ITSAPPRECIATED

If they can't make time to spend with you, it can be an indication of a much greater issue. Quality time is equivalent to a quality relationship and marriage.

MARRY THE ONE WHO PUTS FORTH REAL NOT A FALSE PRETENSE OF WHAT "COULD BE"

Anyone can pretend to be into you but the one who really wants you will be about it, not just talk about it. Their actions will portray the very essence of their intent towards you. You'll always get an "a" for effort but the lifetime reward is priceless.

MARRY THE ONE WHO SHOWS YOU THAT YOU'RE MORE THAN ENOUGH #THECOMPLETEPACKAGE

For your worth to be recognized beyond the fake or false takes a very rare eye which can only come from the one who has been handpicked just for you. Know your worth and value the one who knows it as well.

MARRY THE ONE THAT WILL HOLD YOU BECAUSE YOU HAD A BAD DAY ALTHOUGH YOU UPSET THEM GREATLY EARLIER IN THE DAY.

Love should be unconditional and should not be based on feelings. Love looks beyond faults to show concern even in the moments of disagreements. Can you love me when you don't like me? That is the question.

MARRY THE ONE WHO TRULY WANTS YOU (COMMITMENT) AND NOT JUST THE AVAILABILITY (CONVENIENCE) OF YOU.

The pursuit is real but consistency and commitment has lacked tremendously when it comes to true partnership and marriage. Do you really want to be with me or just the parts that make life convenient for you? To commit is a promise which turns into a covenant before god.

MARRY THE ONE WHO SMELLS YO' STANK FEET AND STILL RUBS THEM TO MAKE YOU FEEL BETTER

This is the epitome of true love. First of all, feet is not typically the part of the body that anyone wants to rub (wink wink) but if they do after they have been submerged in shoes all day and surface with a not so good odor, you better keep them. Lol

MARRY THE ONE WHO HAS BEEN IN THE TRENCHES WITH YOU. THEY ARE YOUR TRUE SUPPORT AND GENUINELY HAVE YOUR BACK.

No bandwagon-ers allowed!!! If you were overlooked based on status that is not love. The one who saw what god sees and went through the process without understanding but loved you and stood by you should be a definite keeper! Most flee when they do not understand what is on the inside of you.

MARRY THE ONE WHO WON'T CONDEMN YOU IN YOUR WEAKNESS

ROMANS 8:1 KJV

THERE IS THEREFORE NOW NO CONDEMNATION TO THEM WHICH ARE IN CHRIST JESUS, WHO WALK NOT AFTER THE FLESH, BUT AFTER THE SPIRIT.

The bible speaks of not condemning so why would we invoke that upon our significant other who is imperfect? Take the time to communicate areas that need improving and love them to a place of resolution and peace that helps them grow individually and with you.

MARRY THE ONE WHO ONLY WANTS YOUR ATTENTION AND IGNORES THE REST

Plainly put, if they really want you, they will leave the rest alone. No competition or other options needed.

MARRY THE ONE WHO DOES SPECIAL THINGS (BIG OR SMALL) #JUST BECAUSE

Nice gestures are appreciated and does not always require expense. But do them as a way to further express your love and appreciation for the one you have chosen to be with forever.

MARRY THE ONE WHO IS WILLING TO GIVE MORE THAN THEY TAKE

Matthew 5:41 KJV

41 AND WHOSOEVER SHALL COMPEL THEE TO GO A MILE, GO WITH HIM TWAIN.

Limits should not be placed on how far you will go to make your partner happy. Use wisdom of course but to see them smile should be the standard set. Going the extra mile just to bring them joy.

MARRY THE ONE WHO YIELDS WITHOUT QUESTION

Colossians 3:18-21 KJV
18 Wives, be submissive to your husbands, as is fitting in the Lord. 19 Husbands, love your wives and don't become bitter against them.

Submissiveness can be a two way street. Both parties have strengths and weaknesses and working together as a team to meet goals can obligate the yielding of both people.

MARRY THE ONE WHO REFUSES TO GIVE UP ON YOU
#THEGODLYYOU #NOTTHEFOOL

For better or worse is the vow made. Often the worse comes sooner than we anticipate but not giving up is the key to making it to "til death do us part." Put in the time, put in the work.

MARRY THE ONE WHO ISN'T LIKE THE REST

Though similarities may be present, there is something especially different about "the one." The way they look at you, smile at you and even touch you, reaches a part of your soul that has never been touched. They exude honesty and authenticity that sends chills all over your body. They are just different.

2 DIFFERENT BACKGROUNDS

BOAZ AND RUTH

EVERY WOMAN AT SOME POINT HAS SAID, "I AM WAITING ON MY BOAZ" OR "CAN GOD SEND ME MY BOAZ." BUT THE STORY OF BOAZ AND RUTH MODELS GOD'S LOVE FOR US. THEIR STORY IS BIGGER THAN LOVE AND AFFECTION BETWEEN TWO PEOPLE.

THEIR STORY SHOWS TWO PEOPLE FROM DIFFERENT BACKGROUNDS, INCLUDING GEOGRAPHICAL, FINANCIAL, AND OVERALL CULTURE COMING TOGETHER FOR THE PURPOSE OF THE KINGDOM. TWO PEOPLE COMING TOGETHER... THAT "COME TOGETHER" PART CAN SOMETIMES BE MISCONSTRUED AS IN LOVE BOTH PARTIES TRY TO REMAIN INDIVIDUALS AND IGNORE "THEN TWO BECAME ONE." THERE WAS A MUTUAL AGREEMENT AND UNDERSTANDING THAT THEY WOULD ENTER EACH OTHER'S WORLDS BUT RUTH EXEMPLIFIES TRUE SUBMISSION IN WANTING TO BE A PART OF GOD'S COMMUNITY OF PEOPLE.

RUTH 3:9 HE SAID, "WHO ARE YOU?" AND SHE ANSWERED, "I AM RUTH, YOUR SERVANT. SPREAD YOUR WINGS OVER YOUR SERVANT, FOR YOU ARE A REDEEMER."

THIS KIND OF LOVE ALSO PORTRAYS THE REDEEMING LOVE OF GOD TOWARDS US ALL AND SO WE SHOULD DISPLAY IN EVERYDAY LIFE.

A Prayer for Intimacy in Marriage

Heavenly Father, we ask you today, to strengthen the bonds of both physical and spiritual intimacy in our marriage. We are thankful that you have called husband and wife to intimacy with you first, and intimacy with one another.

Please show us any behavior we have been committing that has been preventing us from entering into a deeper intimate relationship with you and one another. Once trust is broken it can be nearly impossible to regain on our own, however, we know that all things are possible with you God. Heal our hearts, Father, of past hurts and help us to trust in you and one another again.

We thank you right now for increased intimacy in our marriage as we seek to honor you and one another through our marriage covenant. In Jesus' name we pray. Amen!

"For this reason a man will leave his father and mother and be united to his wife, and the two will become one flesh." (Ephesians 5:31 NIV)

Crosswalk.com

MARRY THE ONE WHO MAKES YOU ACT LIKE YOU'RE IN A RELATIONSHIP ALTHOUGH YOU'RE NOT YET

This can only be done when you know the person you are with is the real deal. If they exemplify every attribute that meets or exceeds your needs to the point that no one else matters and it is just the two of you, don't let them go!!! They have exceeded your expectations.

37

MARRY THE ONE WHO WANTS YOU AS MUCH AS YOU WANT THEM

You should never be a take it or leave it. The world shouldn't rotate properly without your presence when you are with the right one. To be wanted and feel wanted can make the impossible, possible in love.

MARRY THE ONE WHO ACKNOWLEDGES YOU PRIVATELY AND PUBLICLY #NOSECRETS PERIOD! POINT! BLANK!

When commitment and love are a part of the relationship, your partner will not care who knows of your existence. They will shout it from the highest mountain because they are willing to make their affections towards you public. There will always be a sense of privacy but never secrecy regarding your place in their life.

You should not be a secret. Being private and being a secret are two totally different things.

MARRY THE ONE WHO DOESN'T TREAT YOU LIKE ALL THE REST

There has to be something about you that differentiates you from previous relationships. Your mate will never treat you as they have treated others. In fact, they will treat you better.

MARRY THE ONE WHO POURS JUST AS MUCH INTO AS YOU DO THEM. THEY'RE THE REAL MVP
#ITSNEEDED #ITSAPPRECIATED

Your goals, dreams, aspirations, spiritual well-being and all that concerns you should concern them as well. Your being okay should be a priority and they should nurture all things pertaining to you as much, if not more, as you do for them.

MEN: MARRY THE WOMAN WHO RECOGNIZES AND ACKNOWLEDGES THAT YOU'RE HER HEAD AND HELPS YOU AS A WIFE SHOULD. #SHESAKEEPER

WOMEN: MARRY THE MAN WHO RECOGNIZES AND ACKNOWLEDGES THAT YOU'RE HIS RIB AND HE LEADS YOU PROPERLY. #HESAKEEPER

Proverbs 31 & Ephesians 5:21-33 KJV

Depicts proper order in the house. There is an exchange of submission between a man and a woman. Both parties must understand their role in order for the house to flow properly and smoothly always with God leading.

41

MARRY THE ONE WHO KNOWS THEIR ROLE...

Her role is to help him without minimizing him. His role is to cover her without smothering her. It is a great responsibility. Be with the one who is up for the challenge.

MARRY THE ONE WHO YOU'D LIKE TO SPEND FOREVER WITH #MARRIAGEGOALS

There should never be a question whether or not you'd want to spend forever with your partner. If you can't fathom life without them, be sure to make them a forever partner under god's covenant.

MARRY THE ONE WHO IS SPONTANEOUS
#KEEPITINTERESTING #ADVENTUROUS

Please sir please ma'am - keep it interesting!!! Spontaneity is a must to keep the marriage vibrant and alive. Don't lose the fire even after time passes. Plan impromptu dates and travel. Just because gifts and dinners are a plus and a must!

MARRY THE ONE WHO REMEMBERS THE FIRST DAY YOU MET AND WHAT YOU WERE WEARING

This would just be adorable but indeed not a necessity or make or break! But if they remembered the when, where and what of your first encounter then they should be a keeper!

MARRY THE ONE WHO HAS THE BUILD AN EMPIRE MINDSET

Your life journey with a partner should include kingdom building as well as financial stability. Growth and acceleration should be a part of the process long term. Be equal in state of mind. Who actually remembers this? But if they do, keep them around. This is a cute definition of love at first sight when every detail can be recalled.

MARRY THE ONE WHO PUSHES YOU INTO GREATNESS HARDER THAN YOU WANT TO BE PUSHED

If your partner sees potential and greatness in you and calls that person forth, love them hard. This usually means they see you through the eyes of god and knows your ability beyond what you can see.

MARRY THE ONE WHO LOVES YOU WITH NO STRINGS ATTACHED

If they can love you just because, you have something truly special. They only want to love you and please you expecting nothing in return; meaning their heart is huge.

MARRY THE ONE WHO UNDERSTANDS THEIR ROLE BEFORE MARRIAGE #PRACTICEMAKESPERFECT

One should always be preparing to be their greatest person prior to meeting "the one." But to be intentional in this process yields a great return for both parties. Know who you are and your role.

MARRY THE ONE WHO IS QUALIFIED AND PREPARED TO TAKE CARE OF YOUR HEART

Everyone should not have access to your heart but unfortunately, we give free reign to those inadequate of handling this prized possession. There will be someone who will understand the value and cover your heart in prayer and in love.

MARRY THE ONE WHO MAKES AN INDELIBLE IMPRINT ON YOUR HEART WITHOUT TRYING

The person who just steps in and steps up without any false pretenses should leave a lasting imprint of what love is. Never wanting to misuse or abuse your heart. They understand the "handle with care" instruction and will do so gladly and boldly.

MARRY THE ONE WHO IS AN ASSET NOT A LIABILITY

II Corinthians 6:14 KJV
Be ye not unequally yoked together with unbelievers: for what fellowship hath righteousness with unrighteousness? and what communion hath light with darkness?

Be ye equally yoked... people are assigned to our lives but hopefully our forever partner will come to add and not subtract.

MARRY THE ONE WHO ONLY WANTS TO SEE THE WORLD WITH YOU

Their eyes should not see beyond what you offer and bring. Though individuality in life is permissible, your significant other should have the mindset to experience all things LIFE with you!

MARRY THE ONE WHO WILL NOT LET ANOTHER BEAT THEM SAYING GOOD MORNING

This may seem a bit impossible because who can truly see this through morning after morning. However, the effort is recognized and appreciated. The "Good Morning" phase is still ever-present. When someone wakes and you are the second person on their mind (after Christ), being the first to acknowledge you with a greeting shows they woke up with you on their mind and wanted you to know it. Don't brush that behavior off.

MARRY THE ONE WHO WILL PUT IT ALL ON THE LINE JUST FOR YOU

Can you imagine having someone in your world who will sacrifice for you? Not those things that go against character and integrity but the risky stuff like rejection, heartbreak, lack of reciprocity, just name a few but they deem you worth the risk.

OH! What a feeling?!?!

MARRY THE ONE WHO HAS ALREADY PRAYED FOR YOU BEFORE EVER KNOWING YOU EXISTED

Simply put, this is a sign that preparation was taking place because usually while they were praying for you, they were praying for themselves as well in order to be ready to receive you properly. This relationship/marriage is going to be off the chain especially if both of you were praying.

MARRY THE ONE WHO IS ATTACHED TO YOUR PURPOSE AND DESTINY

Knowing what you are called to do is a great feeling but when God connects you to someone with a separate purpose but separately the two of you complement one another for "The Ultimate Purpose" designed by God, nothing will ever be more fulfilling and the love created is unexplainable.

MARRY THE ONE WHO IS CONSISTENT

Consistency breeds security on all levels. It brings a certain "in sync" effect allowing both people to know exactly what to expect and how to move accordingly. Greater things come in a consistent environment!

MARRY THE ONE WHO DOESN'T MIND YOU SLOBBERING ALL OVER THEIR ARM WHILE CUDDLING

Okay so this is really nasty but it happens. Don't trip just expect it and accept it. LOL ☺

MARRY THE ONE WHO WILL LOVE YOU THROUGH YOUR PAST

Sometimes we bring issues from our past into the present but I am reminded of a quote I heard that says, "Everyone comes with baggage. Find someone who loves you enough to help you unpack." Unknown

MARRY THE ONE WHO WAKES UP TO CHECK ON YOU IN THE MIDDLE OF THE NIGHT THEN SLAMS YOU WITH A PILLOW SHOT TO THE HEAD

#JUSTKIDDING #ITSGONBEAFIGHT

Pillow Fight!!! Stop being so serious. It will be fun. Just try it. It will definitely keep things interesting. LOL

MARRY THE ONE WHO WILL SKIP WORK JUST TO PLAY FOOTSIES AND WATCH NETFLIX ALL DAY
#NOELECTRONICDEVICES #UNINTERRUPTEDATTENTION

It really is about time and attention. Sometimes those spur of the moment events can calm doubt, eliminate insecurity, bring joy and peace and extend an insurmountable love between two people. Make the moments count and make them happen as often as possible.

MARRY THE ONE WHO IS IMPERFECTLY PERFECT

They should not have to be perfect to experience a God kind of love. We all come with flaws and varying imperfections just make sure you walk through them together perfectly, without judgement or discord.

MARRY THE ONE WHO WILL NOT LET ANOTHER EXCEED THEM IN EFFORTS OF MAKING YOU FEEL SPECIAL

It is important that you meet one another in the middle especially when it comes to efforts. Gary Chapman who wrote "The Five Love Languages" provided a cheat sheet for us all. Use it!!! Efforts take place in various ways. Just read the book and ask your partner.

3 CULTURAL DIFFERENCES

ESTHER AND XERXES

ANOTHER EXAMPLE OF DIFFERENT PEOPLE, DIFFERENT BACKGROUNDS…

ESTHER WAS THE SECOND WIFE OF KING XERXES AFTER HE CAST HIS FIRST WIFE VASHTI ASIDE. BUT THERE WAS GREAT PURPOSE IN THEIR UNION. THERE WAS A PLAN IN PLACE TO KILL ALL JEWS IN PERSIA BUT ONCE DISCOVERED, MORDECAI COUNTERED THAT PLAN UTILIZING ESTHER'S INFLUENCE WITH THE KING TO PREVENT THIS ATTACK AND IT WORKED.

THIS STORY IS ONE THAT PROVES THAT OUR CONNECTIONS, EVEN IN LOVE HAVE PURPOSE. GOD HAS AND WILL JOIN TO PEOPLE TOGETHER FOR KINGDOM PURPOSES. OUR GOAL IN OUR SINGLENESS AND IN MARRIAGE SHOULD BE TO DRAW OTHERS TO GOD, THROUGH LOVE, SO GOD WILL ALWAYS BE GLORIFIED.

PURPOSE SHOULD BE CONSIDERED BEFORE LOVE BETWEEN TWO PEOPLE. THE QUESTION CAN THEY COMPLEMENT THE CALL GOD HAS ON MY LIFE AND OUR SPIRITUAL GIFTS WORK HAND IN HAND TO ACCOMPLISH THE WILL OF GOD IN THE EARTH?

LOVE CAN CONQUER ALL ESPECIALLY WHEN BOTH ARE COMMITTED TO THE ULTIMATE PURPOSE AND GOAL OF CHRIST.

A Prayer for Honesty in Marriage

Father God we come before you today to ask you to help us do everything with absolute honesty in our marriage. Sanctify us by your truth - your word is truth (John 17:17). Help us to never lie to one another. Help us to come clean if we mess up or make a mistake that can affect our marriage - no matter how bad we may feel or embarrassed we may be. Give us the ability to be completely transparent with one another regardless of how we feel.

We thank you for the discernment to know your truth and the conviction to call on the name of Jesus. If there is anything that we have been untruthful about in the past, please help us to share it with one another and give us the wisdom to work through it. We thank you for helping us to be honest as we choose to submit to your spirit. In Jesus' name we pray. Amen.

"Do not lie to each other, since you have taken off your old self with its practices and have put on the new self, which is being renewed in knowledge in the image of its Creator."(Colossians 3:9-10 NIV)

Crosswalk.com

LADIES: MARRY THE MAN WHO WILL LOVE, COVER AND PROTECT YOU AT ALL COSTS.

MEN: MARRY THE WOMAN WHO WILL LOVE, ENCOURAGE AND PRAY FOR YOU WHEN THE REST OF THE WORLD FORGETS.

The truth of the matter is that you should never stop lifting one another up. Your assignment is to always cater to one another in every way. The end result will always cause you both to excel in life and in love with each other.

MARRY THE ONE WHO WANTS TO SHARE EXPERIENCES AND ADVENTURES WITH YOU

All work and no play is absolutely, positively BORING!!! Spice it up!! Try things together that you have never tried before individually or collectively. Have FUN!!! Life is not all about work and there should be balance to know that it is okay to enjoy the fruits of your labor. Get to planning!!!

MARRY THE ONE WHO GIVES WITHOUT LIMITS OR EXPECTATIONS

It is quite easy to overthink what should be given and what should be held back especially before marriage. Truth is be ALL or NOTHING! Live life on the edge a little when it comes to love. There is no harm in proceeding full speed ahead while guarding your heart but please do not hold back out of fear.

JUST DO IT!!!

MARRY THE ONE WHO RECOGNIZES YOUR PAIN BUT MAKES EVERY EFFORT TO LET YOU BE VULNERABLE WITHOUT JUDGEMENT

Have you ever experienced being completely open and honest with someone and they accepted you anyway. As a matter of fact, they pulled it out of you, lovingly. Took you outside of your own mind and thoughts so you could lead with your heart and not fear or mind first.

MARRY THE ONE WHO CHASES AFTER GOD FIRST

The person who chases after God first will always be led by God. Therefore, there will be no room for error individually, in relationship or marriage. That statement does not mean you will not experience trials and tribulations but if God is your first source and resource, find peace in the fact that ALL will be well. As we pursue god, our ultimate goal should always be to meet god even through the one we love. There must be a standard set through every aspect of getting to know someone through marriage that god will always be the focus. It is in this that two individuals can love in oneness.

MARRY YOUR PROMISE

God identifies our partner in His Word. He promises us a particular man or woman according to scriptures Ephesians 5 and proverbs 31. Look for those attributes to the promises of God for your spouse.

MARRY THE ONE WHO IS YOUR EVERYTHING

To be clear, this does not mean that you idolize or worship your spouse. However, because you have been joined in marriage after being led by the Holy Spirit, nothing or no one should take precedence over the covenant you have with God or with each other.

MARRY THE ONE GOD HAS ORDAINED FOR YOUR LIFE

I do believe that God has a specific type of person for our lives. That special someone who gives us butterflies, causes our eyes to twinkle, and our heart to flutter. However, the true testament comes when all those things fade and you are left staring at the rawest and realest structure of the human you have vowed to love forever. God will show you even when the "honeymoon" phase is over.

MARRY THE ONE WHO MAKES IT EASY TO BE YOU

You should not have to stunt or pretend to be anyone other than your best you. The one who embraces you as YOU is to be loved without questions. Just make sure that you are just as accepting.

MARRY THE ONE WHO LOVES THE THICK, CHUNKY YOU

Society has already placed stigma on how we should look and carry ourselves just to fit in. Your partner should not be a part of the foolery. They should accept you size, status and silliness.

MARRY THE ONE WHO OPENS WIDE THEIR HEART

2 CORINTHIANS 6:11-13 KJV
11 O ye Corinthians, our mouth is open unto you, our heart is enlarged. 12 Ye are not straitened in us, but ye are straitened in your own bowels. 13 Now for a recompense in the same, (I speak as unto my children,) be ye also enlarged.

To give love liberally, requires opening your heart WIDE!!! No reservation or hesitation. The experience is so worth it. Imagine how WIDE God's heart is open to us...

It is so beautiful!!!

MARRY THE ONE WHO WILL TAKE CARE OF YOU WHEN IT REALLY COUNTS. WITHOUT YOU ASKING

When you are in sync with the Holy Spirit and one another, "to-do" should never be a question. If you see there is a need and you are able to meet the need, then just do it. You will be appreciated for it and if married hopefully rewarded as well. ☺

MARRY THE ONE WHO WANTS THE INTANGIBLE PARTS OF YOU

So, it is one thing to admire someone for beauty and prestige, but can you look beyond what you see and tap into that next level intimacy? Focusing on the mind, heart and spirit; even those things unspoken and unseen.

MARRY THE ONE WHO WANTS TO JUST HOLD YOU UNTIL YOU FEEL BETTER

Life will have its moments where it will knock the wind out of us and the time may come where health issues arise. The one that is willing and available to go through those seasons with you only wants the best for you.

MARRY THE ONE WHO'S DESIRE IS TO MAKE YOUR DREAMS AND VISIONS COME TO PASS

The person that can see your visions and dreams and step right in and walk with you to achieve them even without you having to coerce them is God sent. Pay attention and do not let them go. Not now or EVER!

MARRY THE ONE WHO MISSES YOU ALTHOUGH YOU'RE IN THE NEXT ROOM

So sweet! What you share with someone does not need to be explained because it is understood. A connection like this is rare but attainable. Find it!!!

MARRY THE ONE WHO LOVES YOU LIKE YOU LOVE

Let me clarify…

Though the method in which they love will be different, it will be with same thought, passion, enthusiasm, excitement, even extreme that you love. The common goal will always have you in mind.

Male and Female alike.

MARRY THE ONE WHO ASSISTS YOU IN SHARPENING THE GIFTS GOD HAS CALLED YOU TO RATHER THAN CRITICIZING THEM

We are all called to proclaim the gospel of Jesus Christ and blessed with gifts that assists the body of Christ while glorifying God. The one who can walk with you through the process of walking in your calling even when they do not understand, is called to your walk and calling. You will be able to identify them based upon their being in tune with the Holy Spirit and you.

MARRY THE ONE WHO UNDERSTANDS THAT WHAT I SAID DIDN'T CHANGE BECAUSE YOU CHANGED, I MEANT IT. #VOWS

Hebrews 13:8 KJV
He is the same yesterday, today and forever.

True love never loses its flavor, favor or grace upon the one you professed to love for life. Days will come when you feel as though you do not know who you are connected to but even in their changes, your love will remain the same as Christ's love for us remain the same.

MARRY THE ONE WHO SEES YOU THE WAY GOD SEES YOU #THEGOOD #THEBAD #THEUGLY #LOVESYOUSTILL #UNCONDITIONALLY

That saying, "I love them all the way down to their dirty drawls," exemplifies the depth in which you "SEE" someone yet still love them.

MARRY THE ONE WHO STANDS BY YOU PUBLICLY BUT CORRECTS YOUR WRONG PRIVATELY. #PROTECTIVE

Right or Wrong, they will hold you down to the world but as soon as you get home... It will be on and popping!!! Like, what in the world were you thinking? But I still love you!

MARRY THE ONE WHO DOES THAT THING NO ONE ELSE HAS EVER DONE IN YOUR LIFE

Time, thought and consideration will get you EVERYTHING!!! Take the time to be what no one has ever been to your partner. The connection grows when you consider one another at all times.

MARRY THE ONE WHO DOESN'T PLAY GAMES AT ALL

Cat and mouse has become the norm for many situations or seeing who's going to make the first move or putting someone in rotation to earn a spot. Games cause pain. If there is not an interest initially, then let the situation go. The "One" will recognize you as the MVP and come out of the game to get you.

MARRY THE ONE WHO HAS A MIND OF THEIR OWN BUT WILL COMPROMISE FOR THE SAKE OF THE HOUSEHOLD #TEAMWORK #DREAMWORK

Being right should never be the thought process of either partner but determining the best possible solution for the entire house should always be the focus. It is okay to have a variance in thought but to do what is best for all takes humility and maturity.

MARRY THE ONE WHO LOVES YOU BUT WILL RELEASE YOU TO YOUR HAPPINESS #DONTLETTHEMGO #THATSREALLOVE

WE have the tendency to hold on to people that we should probably release but due to invested time, money and emotions, we stay hoping things will change and get better. The true art of love is releasing someone to heal, love again or just be free!!! It hurts but you will both be glad you did.

Love prevails always!!!

MARRY THE ONE WHO PRAYED AND PREPARED JUST FOR YOU EVEN BEFORE THEY MET YOU #THEYAREREADY #SOAREYOU

This can be deemed as a true sign of a person truly waiting and relying on God to match them with the perfect mate for life. If both persons are preparing, the wait is worth journey ahead.

MARRY THE ONE WHO WON'T HAVE YOU OUTCHEA IN THESE STREETS LOOKING CRAZY

Real life...

Every person reading this knows exactly what I mean when I say "outchea in these streets looking crazy."

No explanation needed!

MARRY THE ONE WHO YOU TRUST COMPLETELY

Trust is earned. Although no one can ever really know if trust will be broken but the one who is willing to earn your trust even if it hurts and especially by telling you the truth at all costs, should be trusted.

MARRY THE ONE WHO YOU CAN BUILD WITH

As with any given situation, there should be a common goal. When connecting with someone the purpose for building the Kingdom of God should be at the top of the list but as well as building a life according to the plan and purpose found in the scripture... the life more abundantly part. Build together, grow together!!!

4 Hopeless Romantic

SONG OF SOLOMON

SONG OF SOLOMON IS ONE BOOK OF THE BIBLE WHICH SHOWCASES LOVE, MARRIAGE AND YES... SEX

THE LANGUAGE USED IS SENSUAL BUT PROVIDES THE DEPTH OF LOVE GOD HAS FOR HIS PEOPLE. GOD INVENTED ALL OF THE ABOVE AS A BLESSING AND IT IS HIS WILL THAT HIS PEOPLE ENJOY HIS BLESSINGS IN ITS RIGHT CONTEXT.

IT OPENS WITH THIS SHULAMMITE WOMAN LONGING TO BE KISSED BY HER KING AND HE IN RETURN IS FOND OF HER BUT SONG OF SOLOMON 2:7 GIVES INSTRUCTIONS TO WAIT UNTIL MARRIAGE. IT FOLLOWS GOD'S ORDER FOR A HUSBAND AND WIFE. WE FIND TODAY THAT THE WAITING PROCESS CAN BE EXTREMELY DIFFICULT ESPECIALLY WHEN THE MIND, BODY AND SOUL YEARNS TO BE LOVED AND TOUCHED. OFTEN TIMES, MATTERS ARE TAKEN INTO OUR OWN HANDS THEREFORE IN THE END LOVE LOSES.

THIS BOOK OF THE BIBLE CAPTURES EVERY ASPECT OF BEING SINGLE, DATING, BEING ENGAGED AND LASTLY MARRIAGE. IT DEPICTS WHAT THAT LOOKS LIKE FOR A BELIEVER. IT IS A DEEP BOND THAT CONSISTS OF FRIENDSHIP, INTIMACY, ENDURANCE AND COMMITMENT. THERE ARE INDEED LESSONS IN THIS STORY THAT COINCIDE WITH GOD'S LOVE FOR THE CHURCH.

TO BE CONTINUED...

Prayer for a Christ-Centered Marriage

Today, we give our marriages to You. Forgive us for putting them and our spouses before You. Forgive us for putting ourselves as well as our desires and plans for the future before You and Yours.

Search our hearts, Lord. Convict us and clear out all the hardness and ick that is clogging up the flow of Love in our lives. Reset our relationship with You. Restore our hope in Jesus Christ and open our minds and hearts to the healing truth that only He can rush into our lives in these moments of madness.

Give us the strength to be brave. Replace the fear of what might happen and what the future might hold with Christ-centered courage. We can't be strong right now. We are broken and barely breathing. But You, the living God, in us, are our strength.

Through the Holy Spirit of the One True God, empower us with humility, gentleness, patience, peace, and unity (Ephesians 4:2-3).

Curb our anger from morphing into bitterness and hatred. Forgive us for the times we lose our tempers and our sanity towards our spouse.

Even if you are not in the habit of praying, that can change. We encourage those of you who do not regularly pray to start with committing to pray once a day. Some of the best times to pray are the times that you are doing something essential. Amen. - Meg Bucher

crosswalk.com

MARRY THE ONE WHO MAKES YOU FEEL NEEDED AND WANTED AS WELL
#THEREISADIFFERENCE
#ITMAKESADIFFERENCE

Being with someone based on need can be mistaken as being taken advantage of. However, to need someone to grow in purpose is preferred. The desire of a person (want) extends further than the need. When relationship gets to the "I need you and I want you" it is inevitable that something special will be birthed. Go for the need and the want.

MARRY THE ONE WHO HAS A GLOBAL MINDSET FOR YOUR HOUSEHOLD
#EMPIREBUILDING#TEAMWORK #DREAMWORK

Acts 1:8

[8] but ye shall receive power, after that the holy ghost is come upon you: and ye shall be witnesses unto me both in Jerusalem, and in all Judaea, and in Samaria, and unto the uttermost part of the earth.

Because God wants to blow our mind, our mind should be set on Him and all that He desires to do in our lives globally for His glory. Our thoughts individually and collectively should be to reach the nations in ministry but in business. Create a legacy that benefits everyone. Bless the nations with your gifts.

MARRY THE ONE WHO HEARS YOUR HEART

Words unspoken, speak the loudest. For they come from the heart and soul. Words that cannot be expressed verbally. To be so in tune with someone that you feel, hear and know their heart is the truest expression of listening to your partner and becoming one. Can you hear them even when they do not speak???

MARRY THE ONE WHO WILL LOVE YOU EVEN WHEN IT'S DIFFICULT TO LOVE YOU

1 Corinthians 13:4-8; 13 NIV

4 Love is patient, love is kind. It does not envy, it does not boast, it is not proud. 5 It does not dishonor others, it is not self-seeking, it is not easily angered, it keeps no record of wrongs. 6 Love does not delight in evil but rejoices with the truth. 7 It always protects, always trusts, always hopes, always perseveres. 8 Love never fails. 13 And now these three remain: faith, hope and love. But the greatest of these is love.

MARRY THE ONE WHO RECOGNIZES YOUR IMPERFECTIONS BUT LOVES YOU ANYWAY WHILE EXPOSING THEIR OWN IMPERFECTIONS SO YOU BOTH CAN LEARN AND GROW TOGETHER

Matthew 7:3-5 KJV

3 "Why do you look at the speck of sawdust in your brother's eye and pay no attention to the plank in your own eye? 4 How can you say to your brother, 'Let me take the speck out of your eye,' when all the time there is a plank in your own eye? 5 You hypocrite, first take the plank out of your own eye, and then you will see clearly to remove the speck from your brother's eye.

Do this in love and respect so both persons can learn and grow.

MARRY THE ONE WHO CHOOSES YOU EVERYDAY

To be with someone and be committed is a choice. To make this decision daily with so many options in the world takes integrity and maturity. There will be bad days, so the decision to pack up and leave is an easy out but the decision to stay is hard but shows heart! Choose wisely!!!

MARRY THE ONE WHO WILL CHANGE YOUR LIFE FOREVER

There will come a day when you will meet the person who will completely change your vision, perspective and thoughts therefore changing your life for the better. They will be the person that you will never be able to forget.

MARRY THE ONE WHO MAKES YOU BETTER

If they make you think greater, feel greater, live greater then, they are making you better. No excuses just true passion and devotion to get you to your best life.

MARRY THE ONE WHO WANTS TO SEE YOU EVOLVE INTO GREATNESS

Similar to the previous MT1, the person that wants to walk through your evolution into greatness with you, never giving up on you is a gift. Cherish them because they will see your losses and your wins and will love you through each and every last one picking you up and dusting you off.

MARRY THE ONE WHO WILL ROAST YOU ALL DAY BUT LET SOMEONE ELSE SAY SOMETHING CRAZY ABOUT YOU AND IT WILL BE WAR!!!

Wait!!! What did you say about my Bae??? Oh, you just went too far. I can talk about them all day but you need to watch your words.

That's Bae!!! LOL

MARRY THE ONE WHO CHANGES YOUR LIFE WITHOUT EVEN TRYING

The way they smile at you and more importantly the way you smile back will be an indicator of a life changer in love. They will make you feel as if a part of you has been missing your entire life. You will know them by how they change your mind, soul and your heart. Nothing before them, hurt, disappointment, or fear will matter. You will only consider your future with them and the changes the two of you will now make together.

MARRY THE ONE WHO MAKES LIFE EASIER WHEN LIFE IS HARDEST

They will not add stress to your day but will please you in every way. You are excites to share your day even if it has been the worst day. You have confidence that they will listen and somehow make everything okay. The world will be better now that you are with them. This kind of love comes easy. Not without issues but it does not offer pain either.

MARRY THE ONE WHO BRINGS YOU PEACE OF MIND, PEACE IN HEART AND PEACE IN YOUR SPIRIT #PEACEMATTERS

Drama will be the farthest thing on their mind. They walk in peace and contentment and they will strive to offer that vibe to you as well. Picking fights or arguments will never be their agenda but to offer a place of serenity that always feel like home is the standard.

MARRY THE ONE WHO CONSIDERS YOU BEFORE THEY CONSIDER THEMSELVES
#IFITBENEFITSONE #ITBENEFITSBOTH

To be thought of first, speaks volumes about the person professing to love you without limits or boundaries. This showcases a love that is selfless. Selfless love is one of the greatest kinds of love.

MARRY THE ONE WHO YOU CAN'T GET RID OF BECAUSE THEY'RE ENGRAFTED IN YOUR LIFE DEEPLY #SPIRITHEARTMIND #DAY2DAY #FOREVER

Soulmate equates to a life mate. They are someone as the dictionary describes as ideally suited to another as a close friend or romantic partner. You don't have to explain yourself because from day one they just get you. You are totally free to be who you are and they understand your feelings and thoughts and can even finish your sentences. They are your perfect match.

MARRY THE ONE WHO TELLS YOU HOW NICE YOU LOOK OFTEN. NOT BECAUSE YOU NEED THAT BUT BECAUSE THEY BELIEVE THAT.
#SIMPLETHINGS
#COMPLIMENTEACHOTHER

We have learned that words of affirmation go a long way. It is indeed one of the "Five Love Languages." But you should always notice the beauty of your partner from an external perspective and internally as well. "Beauty is in the eye of the beholder" was first used by Margaret Wolfe Hungerford in 1878 and could not be more true. Most will not see what you see in a person and that is usually because you are viewing that person from a place that isn't surface but depth.

MARRY THE ONE WHO LOVES YOU UNCOMPLICATED

There have been many statuses regarding love being complicated which is so far from the truth. Love is simple just do it. However, it is the action of people that complicate it. Choose someone who is willing to fight for love in its simplest nature and remove any complications to reach the fullest potential of love unconditional.

MARRY THE ONE WHO WILL BE THERE WHEN YOU'RE AT YOUR LOWEST SO THEY CAN HELP YOU RISE AGAIN #A4LIFEKINDALOVE

The key word in this phrase is "HELP." To have someone willing to help you even when they need help is someone going the extra mile. We are not looking for you to choose someone to use but someone to join forces and excel together.

MARRY THE ONE WHO WANTS TO LIVE IN THE MOMENT WITH YOU

No moment is promised so live each one as if it is the last one. Don't ever leave a moment having not given your all. Don't hold back as you may regret it later.

MARRY THE ONE WHO DATES YOU #ITSANEXPERIENCE

The goal is to make memories through great conversation and adventure. Make every date count. Memories last forever!!!

MARRY THE ONE WHO TALKS TO GOD ABOUT YOU #COVEREDBYHISBLOOD #THATSLOVE

Ooooweeee…

To have a love like this where God is consulted with all things concerning you shows deep love. It gives reverence to God then honor to you. This brings a certain kind of closeness to our Father and between both persons involved. Seek God first.

MARRY THE ONE WHO POURS JUST AS MUCH INTO YOU AS YOU DO THEM #DONTLEAVETHEMEMPTY

We usually give up parts of ourselves to others which can turn out to be exhausting for us in every way imaginable. Though it can change the life of the other person, it can leave you depleted. Those who take without ever giving back should be considered temporal in your life because in some cases once they have what they need to feel better, move or grow they will leave you empty. But the one who desires to give just as much as you give, brings a sense of wholeness, fulfillment, and a new found hope of what is ahead.

MARRY THE ONE WHO CAN PUT THE PIECES OF YOUR LIFE BACK TOGETHER.

This person can help reassemble the broken pieces that once took over your life mainly because they actually have the pieces you need to do so. Certain devastations can consume us and yes we have a responsibility to heal and grow on our own but to have someone who can assist you through the process are keepers of the peace and pieces of your life too. Embrace them and their love.

MARRY THE ONE WHO WILL FIGHT4U!!!

"I am a lover, not a fighter," no ma'am, no sir, I am both especially if you mess with what is mine. Don't come for Bae!!! It will not be good. Hopefully, y'all recognize that I am not speaking of literally because you can catch case but understand defending that which you love by any means necessary is vital. But if you push well...

Where are my boxing gloves???

MARRY THE ONE WHO UNDERSTANDS THAT MARRIAGE IS MINISTRY!!! #FLESHOFMYFLESH #BONEOFMYBONE

When God places the life of another in your hands, your job is to minister there. You serve God first then exercise your vows towards one another and serve your spouse. Your catering to your spouse benefits both of you.

5 A SACRIFICIAL LOVE

JESUS ON THE CROSS

WHAT DOES LOVE REALLY LOOK LIKE? IS IT THE NICE GESTURES OR KIND WORDS? TEXTING OR CALLING? SPENDING QUALITY TIME? LOVE OVER TIME HAS BEEN PORTRAYED IN WAYS OF, IF YOU DO THIS YOU LOVE ME. LOVE IS UNDOUBTEDLY – SACRIFICE!!! THE GREATEST EXAMPLE WE HAVE IS JESUS ON THE CROSS FOR EACH OF US. ALTHOUGH HE WAS FULLY AWARE THAT WE ARE IMPERFECT AND WOULD MESS UP EVEN THOUGH HE GAVE UP HIS LIFE FOR OURS. BUT YET HE DID IT!!! YET HE ACCEPTS US!!!

THERE IS NO GREATER LOVER THAN A MAN LAY DOWN HIS LIFE FOR A FRIEND – JOHN 15:13

THIS IS THE TYPE OF LOVE WE SHOULD SEEK IN MARRIAGE. ACCEPTING ONE ANOTHER FOR WHO WE ARE AND LOVING IN SPITE OF. IT IS TOTAL COMMITMENT AND SELFLESSNESS. IT DOES NOT SEEK RECIPROCITY.

LOVE JUST IS!! LOVE JUST DOES!!!

Prayer for Forgiveness in Marriage

Heavenly Father, as we strive to continuously build a stronger marriage, help us to forgive one another for things that may hurt or offend us. Help us to walk in forgiveness and never lose sight of the fact that you have forgiven us.

Help us to show your mercy and grace to our spouse each time they need it and not bring up past hurts or failures. Let us be an example of forgiveness to not only our spouse but to those around us so we can continue to show your love to all we meet. Help us to also forgive ourselves if we struggle with condemnation.

Thank you for your life-giving words of truth that we may be redeemed by the blood of the Lamb. In Jesus' name we pray. Amen!

"If we confess our sins, he is faithful and just and will forgive us our sins and purify us from all unrighteousness." (1 John 1:9 NIV)

crosswalk.com

MARRY THE ONE WHO LISTENS

Listening is essential to a healthy marriage. To lose the ability to communicate effectively can turn into nagging or hurtful words trying to get a point across. There should be liberty in being heard and understood whether agreed or not and punishment should never be the response when it's something you don't want to hear. Effectiveness in listening can open doors of power within your marriage for both to grow. Besides this covenant we call marriage is a forever situation.

MARRY THE ONE WHOSE EFFORTS MATCH YOURS.

Now, this statement is debatable but who doesn't like a good, healthy debate. Effort matching to me, is engagement matching. Are you as equally engaged in cultivating this "something special" we have? Does your interest level in me, match my interest level in you? However, in the game of cat and mouse, the playing fields are never truly equal. I question, "Why even pay the game?" But that's another topic for another time. I will say that relationships and marriages take work therefore, all parties involved should be equally putting their best foot forward. The effort going forth should feel worthwhile for the other person. IT should be satisfying. Don't leave them hanging and desiring more.

MARRY THE ONE WITH WHOM YOU CAN BE NAKED AND UNASHAMED #TRANSPARENT

Can I show you my scars and you not judge me? Can I be completely vulnerable and you not use it against me? When I make a mistake, will you mock me? If I show you my heart, will you play it like a fiddle? Every person wants that one someone with whom all masks and filters come off. Can you be trusted to be that person?

MARRY THE ONE WHO GENUINELY APPRECIATES YOU NOT ONLY IN WORDS BUT IN THEIR ACTIONS #SIMPLETHINGS

Actions speak louder than words. Love can be expressed via the things we not only say but actually do. Make certain your words match your actions.

MARRY THE ONE WHO REFUSES TO LET YOU QUIT

In love, quitting is never an option, whether it is quitting together or individually.

MARRY THE ONE WHO WATCHES THE SUNSET WITH YOU, NOT UTTERING A WORD BUT SIMPLY LISTENING TO THE BEAT OF YOUR HEART AND THE SONG IN YOUR SPIRIT.

This action-less effort is simply enjoying the presence of another person. It does not require much effort just to enjoy being with someone while doing nothing. Melodies should be heard with every breath you take and in every word you speak. It's a musical!!!

MARRY THE ONE WHO WILL TRY AND FAIL WITH YOU BUT GET UP AND TRY AGAIN WITH YOU JUST THE SAME

Someone willing to be there through your wins and losses understands that the true testament of love successful is going through both the good and bad in life but never letting go and never giving up.

MARRY THE ONE WHO SAYS I DO AND I WILL #VOWS

A vow is a promise and the person willing to commit to promises of the covenant should not be denied as long as they actually do and will for all eternity.

MARRY THE ONE WHO IS GRATEFUL TO HAVE YOU

Gratefulness is shown through appreciation. When someone is grateful to have you their level of appreciation for you and all you bring. Their expression of gratefulness unspoken goes beyond virtue it is an attitude towards the one another. It is time put in and practice. This expression of love is intentional.

MARRY THE ONE WHO WILL WALK MILES FOR YOU

The Proclaimers wrote a song "I'm Gonna Be" and his lyrics state…

"But I would walk 500 miles, And I would walk 500 more, Just to be the man who walks a thousand miles." That's love.   What extent are you willing to go to express your love?
#trywalkingfirst

MARRY THE ONE WHO CONSTANTLY FALLS IN LOVE WITH YOU

Finding new reasons and ways to fall in love with you daily can be challenging especially when issues arise. But doing so anyway, showcases a lover ever-defining new meaning.

MARRY THE ONE WHO WANTS TO MARRY YOU

Duh!!! It feels great to be wanted. Be with someone who wants you as much as you want them.

MARRY THE ONE WHO IS HONEST WITH AND ABOUT YOU EVEN WHEN IT HURTS. THEY HAVE YOUR BEST INTEREST AT HEART.

Honesty is the best policy even when it hurts or doesn't want to be heard. Be that one somebody that your partner can trust to always tell them the truth no matter. The truth wins over a lie any day. It is greatly appreciated even if it's after the fact.

MARRY THE ONE WHO… {YOU FILL IN THE BLANK}

6 TRUE REVELATION

GOD AND THE CHURCH

GOD IS LOVE. THOUGH TRUE, IT HAS BECOME COMMON TERMINOLOGY. IF PAINTED ON A CANVAS, HOW WOULD HIS LOVE APPEAR? THE BEST ANSWER, BIBLICAL ANSWER IS CHRIST JESUS HANGING ON A CROSS. THIS IS A FULL EXPLANATION OF HIS AS THE BLOOD OF HIS SON REDEEMS US!!! AS MENTIONED IN THE EARLIER SECTION 'SONG OF SOLOMON' GOD WANTS TO HAVE FRIENDSHIP WITH US, INTIMACY WITH US, ENDURANCE WITH US AND ABOVE ALL ELSE COMMITMENT FROM US. WE SOMETIMES PICK GOD UP WHEN IT'S CONVENIENT FOR US OR IN THE MIDST OF TRIAL. HE'D LOVE TO HAVE THAT AT ALL TIMES. THOUGH HIS GRACE ALLOWS US TO COME AND GO, HIS CHASTISEMENT IN LOVE, CAN ALSO ALLOW GRIEF UPON US.

GOD IS A RELATIONAL GOD AND HIS DESIRE IT TO HAVE RELATIONSHIP WITH US. THE WHOLE PERSON OF JESUS DYING ON THE CROSS AND RISING WAS SO THAT WE COULD CONNECT WITH HIM THROUGH THE BLOOD OF JESUS. ONCE YOU HAVE ACCEPTED JESUS, YOU CAN CONNECT WITH HIM DIRECTLY BECAUSE NOW WHEN HE SEES US, HE SEES THE BLOOD OF HIS ONLY SON!

OUR LOVE IN RELATIONSHIPS HAS TO BLOT OUT TRANSGRESSIONS. IT FORGIVES AND LOVES BEYOND ALL REPROACH!!!

Prayer for Restoration of a Marriage in Trouble

Lord Jesus, nothing seems to be going right in our marriage. Lately, we argue over so many things. Or we walk out in anger or silence, too upset to deal with any issues. Sometimes we fuss about little problems that don't really matter or hide things that really are important. But in Your eyes, Lord, everything matters. Pebbles grow to mountains when they pile up, day after day. When did it all start? Did we retreat into our own worlds? Become too busy to care? Did we stop listening to You and to each other?

Teach us how to communicate—to simply talk to each other again with courtesy and kindness. Show us again what love and respect look like, and what it means to honor and mutually submit to the other as a man and woman in love with You, Lord. We've forgotten all the basics. And we sense that if we don't deal with even small problems now, we'll be facing a much greater roadblock later. Maybe we've forgotten what love is really like.

121

Or maybe we never really knew. Regardless, Lord, our marriage is in trouble. We need you. No matter how difficult the circumstances, we want to face them together—with You on our side. You've told us we would experience troubles on this earth, but that You are the great Overcomer. With You, Lord, we can mend the tears and amend the errors. With You, we can build a successful marriage. In Your name, Amen. - Rebecca Barlow Jordan

crosswalk.com

Prayer for Health for You and Your Spouse

Father God we thank you for divine health in our physical bodies, spiritual life, and marriage. We pray that you will make known to us anything that we are doing that does not directly correlate with healthy living; body, spirit, soul.

Give us the strength to honor you through our bodies as they are the temple of the Lord. Give us the wisdom to continuously build a healthy spiritual life and marriage with you at the center.

Help us to always remember the sacrifice you made that gave us the promise of healing and peace. You are worthy to be praised! In Jesus' name we pray. Amen!

"But he was wounded for our transgressions, he was bruised for our iniquities: the chastisement of our peace was upon him; and with his stripes we are healed." (Isaiah 53:4 KJV)

Prayer for Your Marriage

Father, help me to be the [husband/wife] you have intended me to be. Show me where I need to improve. Help me to be a better communicator, help me to love my [husband/wife] better, and help us both to grow closer to You and to each other in this new year. In Jesus' name, amen. - Brent Rinehart

A Prayer for Love and Joy in Marriage

Dear God, in Your presence we renew our whole-hearted choice to love. Bless this holy commitment with courage, strength, tenacity— and most of all joy! Amen. - Dr. James Dobson

Prayer for a Healed Marriage

Lord, I want our marriage to be healed. Let the healing begin with me. Have mercy on me, Lord, a spouse who has failed so often to demonstrate Your love.

I want to love my spouse the way You love me. Help me. I want to be a vessel of Your love, joy, peace, patience, kindness, goodness, faithfulness, gentleness, and self-control in _____'s life. Use me.

I want to love in such a way that ____ is inspired to praise You. Glorify Yourself in me, Lord. Amen. - Jennifer O. White

crosswalk.com

WORKS CITED

"Bible Hub: Search, Read, Study the Bible in Many Languages." *Bible Hub: Search, Read, Study the Bible in Many Languages*, 2019, biblehub.com/kjv.

Kercheval, Michael, and Carlie Kercheval. "Intersection of Life and Faith." *Crosswalk.com*, June 2018, www.crosswalk.com/.

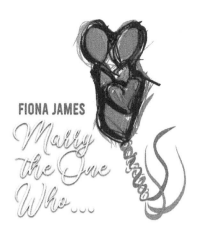

MT1 Trivia Game Answers

1. One head – God
2. Head forms heart = love
3. Two people kissing = intimacy
4. One mind, body, soul connected/interwoven
5. Heart for God and one another
6. Heart serves as arms holding one another up
7. 3 strand cord – Ecc 4:12

...